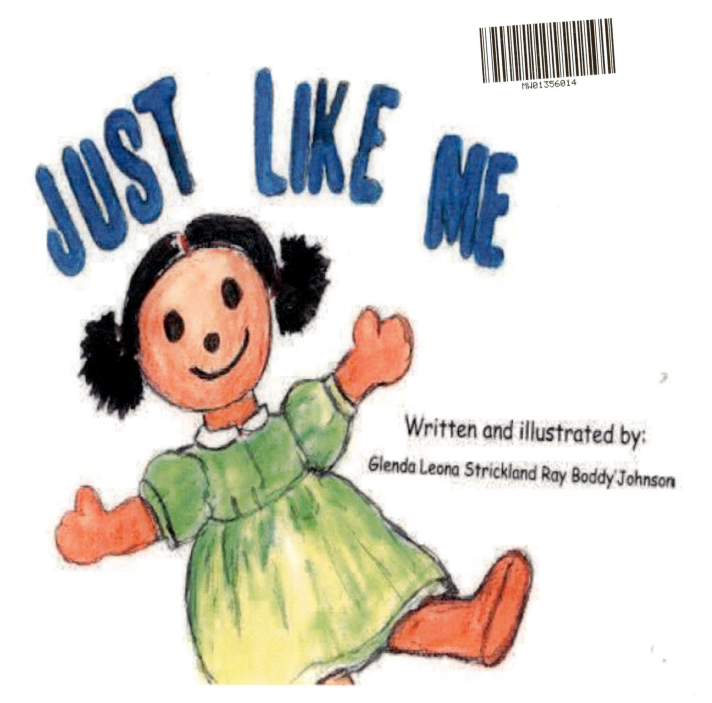

JUST LIKE ME

Written and illustrated by:
Glenda Leona Strickland Ray Boddy Johnson

Copyright © 2023

All Rights Reserved

Dedicated to my sweet Granny

Remembering to never forget

A special thanks to my superman Alim for your love and our beautiful children, "together us."

About the Author

Glenda Leona Strickland Ray Boddy'Johnson is a 71-year-old Native American/African American self-taught artist who paints truths from her childhood memories. She is a lifetime Montessori educator and consultant.

"BJ" was born in Fayetteville, North Carolina, and currently resides and teaches in New York City.

Story Summary

Teeny, a little African-American girl, wishes she had a beautiful doll that looked like her. The story takes place in the 1950s on the cusp of the civil right movement.

We lived on a street called Vanstory in a big yellow house with a green swing on the porch. We had a tree swing in the backyard, too.

Grandpa James put the tree swing up for me. He hung it on the old pecan tree. I loved to swing in it.

My friend Jessica liked to swing on my swing too. Jessica lived across the way. Jessica would bring her dolly to swing with her on my swing.

I wished that I had a beautiful dolly like Jessica. A dolly that looked like me.

I am the color of "French coffee mixed with a little milk chocolate," my grandma Willie Mae says.

Jessica's doll looks like her, she is not milk chocolate like me. We like to play in the backyard when it's not too hot.

On Tuesday, Granny said we were going into town because she had to buy some more thread for her quilting group.

On the way to Mr. Brown's general store, we passed by old Ben's toy store. Old man Ben didn't have a sign in his window that read "Whites Only" like other stores.

Granny said, "Mr. Ben's prices were so high that only white people could afford to buy anything anyway."

When we stood in front of the store, I saw her: the most doll beautiful doll I had ever seen.

She had on a beautiful pink dress, and she had long blonde hair and big blue eyes. It looked like her arms were reaching out for me, as if she wanted me to take her home with me.

There was only one problem: she didn't look like me. My granny says that I am beautiful and that I am her beautiful chocolate baby. Granny says that I am a princess. I want a doll that looks just like me.

I asked Granny if we could go into old man Ben's toy store next time to buy a dolly that looked like me.

Granny said, "Child, you know ol' man Ben doesn't have any dolls that look like you. And even if he did, it would cost too much."

I was sad. I wanted to cry. I felt my head going down, and two tears landed on my shirt.

It was Wednesday, time for the quilting group to come over. I was excited to see my family members. These were people that I had known all my life.

There was Auntie Hattie Mae and Mary Lou. Mary Lou was Granny's half-sister. I don't know how much sister a "half-sister" is yet.

There was CC, my mom's cousin. CC is Indian. There was my great-aunt Daisy. Great Aunt Daisy was so skinny; she said that was because she worked hard in the fields and had no time to get fat.

Finally, there was my grandma Willie Mae.

Everybody sat around in a big circle sewing the quilt. I didn't know who the quilt was for, but it sure was pretty. Granny and Grandma Willie Mae were teaching me how to sew a quilt, too.

Granny threaded the needle for me and told me to be careful. Granny said, "Push the needle in through one side and pull it out through the other side, slowly and carefully."

Granny even gave me an area on the quilt to sew.

"In and out, take your time, be careful," Granny said.

My stitches were really far apart, but my family didn't mind. Granny said that I was doing a good job and that she was proud of me.

I love sitting with my family. I mostly don't know what they are talking about, but they sure do laugh a lot!

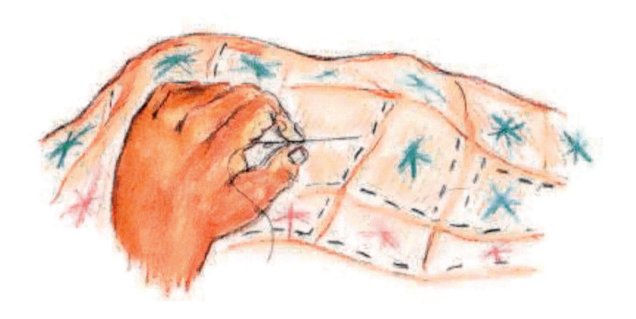

Granny said, "Okay, my girl, it's nap time."

I didn't want to leave them, but I really was sleepy.

When I was sleeping, I dreamed of a beautiful chocolate doll that looked like me with a beautiful purple dress and big black eyes like mine. She would even have curly hair like mine.

Someday, I will have a dolly that looks just like me.

When I woke up from my nap, I went into the room to find Granny.

There, sitting on the table, was a chocolate doll. She was wearing a purple dress, and she had big black eyes. She even had curly hair like mine, and she was smiling at me! Her arms were reaching out for me.

Granny said that my family had made her for me while I was taking a nap.

I love my family, and they love me.

And I love my doll because she looks "just like me."

The End

Made in the USA
Middletown, DE
07 May 2024